contents

NZ, Canada, US and UK readers
Please note that Australian cup and spoon
measurements are metric. A quick conversion
guide appears on page 63.

avocado caprese salad

4 large vine-ripened tomatoes (480g)
250g cherry bocconcini
1 large avocado (320g), halved
¼ cup loosely packed fresh basil leaves
2 tablespoons olive oil
1 tablespoon balsamic vinegar

1 Slice tomato, cheese and avocado thickly.
2 Place slices of tomato, cheese and avocado on serving platter; top with basil leaves, drizzle with combined oil and vinegar. Sprinkle with freshly ground black pepper, if desired.

serves 4
per serving 31.4g fat (10.3g saturated); 1434kJ (343 cal); 2.6g carb
tip Because the tomatoes are being served raw, we used vine-ripened truss tomatoes for their brilliant colour and robust flavour.

thai beef salad

One of everyone's favourites at the local Thai, our version of "yum nuah" is so easy to prepare and so delicious, you'll be making it at home rather than eating it out from now on.

¼ cup (60ml) fish sauce
¼ cup (60ml) lime juice
500g beef rump steak
3 lebanese cucumbers (390g), seeded, sliced thinly
4 fresh small red thai chillies, sliced thinly
4 green onions, sliced thinly
250g cherry tomatoes, halved
¼ cup firmly packed fresh vietnamese mint leaves
½ cup firmly packed fresh coriander leaves
½ cup firmly packed fresh thai basil leaves
1 tablespoon grated palm sugar
2 teaspoons soy sauce
1 clove garlic, crushed

1 Combine 2 tablespoons of the fish sauce and 1 tablespoon of the juice in medium bowl, add beef; toss beef to coat in marinade. Cover; refrigerate 3 hours or overnight.
2 Drain beef; discard marinade. Cook beef on heated oiled grill plate (or grill or barbecue) until cooked as desired. Cover beef, stand 5 minutes; slice beef thinly.
3 Meanwhile, combine cucumber, chilli, onion, tomato and herbs in large bowl.
4 Place sugar, soy sauce, garlic, remaining fish sauce and remaining juice in screw-top jar; shake well. Add beef and dressing to salad; toss gently to combine.

serves 4
per serving 8.7g fat (3.8g saturated); 982kJ (235 cal); 7.9g carb

chicken and rice salad with nam jim dressing

Like most Thai sauces and dressings, nam jim is extremely hot. Seed the chillies to lessen the heat, if you prefer.

1 litre (4 cups) water
600g chicken breast fillets
15cm stick (30g) fresh
    lemon grass
2 star anise
2cm piece fresh ginger (10g),
    sliced thickly
1 tablespoon peanut oil
1 small brown onion (80g),
    chopped finely
1 cup (200g) basmati and
    wild rice mix
300g snow peas, trimmed
1 medium yellow capsicum
    (200g), sliced thinly
150g mizuna
½ cup firmly packed fresh
    coriander leaves
nam jim dressing
10cm stick (20g) fresh lemon
    grass, chopped coarsely
2 cloves garlic, quartered
2 long green chillies,
    chopped coarsely
2 tablespoons lime juice
2 tablespoons peanut oil
1 tablespoon grated
    palm sugar
1 tablespoon fish sauce

1 Bring the water to a boil in medium saucepan; poach chicken, lemon grass, star anise and ginger, covered, about 10 minutes or until chicken is cooked through. Cool chicken in liquid 10 minutes. Strain and reserve cooking liquid; discard lemon grass, star anise and ginger. Slice chicken thinly.
2 Meanwhile, make nam jim dressing.
3 Heat oil in same cleaned saucepan; cook onion, stirring, until soft. Add rice; cook, stirring, 1 minute. Add reserved cooking liquid; bring to a boil. Reduce heat; simmer, uncovered, about 15 minutes or until rice is just tender. Drain; cool 10 minutes.
4 Meanwhile, boil, steam or microwave snow peas until just tender; drain. Rinse under cold water; drain.
5 Place chicken, rice and snow peas in large bowl with capsicum, mizuna, coriander and dressing; toss gently to combine.
nam jim dressing Blend or process ingredients until smooth.

serves 4
per serving 17.9g fat (3.4g saturated); 2031kJ (486 cal); 36.8g carb
tip You can use a barbecued chicken for this recipe; however, you will have to cook the rice in a mixture of water and prepared chicken stock instead of the cooking liquid.

steak and aïoli open sandwiches

Beef sirloin, rib-eye or rump are suitable for this recipe.
Ciabatta is a type of crusty Italian bread.

8 thin beef fillet steaks (800g)
4 large egg tomatoes (360g), halved
1 tablespoon olive oil
½ cup (150g) mayonnaise
1 clove garlic, crushed
4 slices ciabatta
1 tablespoon finely shredded fresh basil
1 tablespoon balsamic vinegar

1 Cook beef and tomato on heated oiled barbecue, uncovered, until beef is browned and cooked as desired. Drizzle tomato with oil; cook until tender.
2 Combine mayonnaise and garlic in small bowl.
3 Toast bread; spread with mayonnaise mixture. Top with beef and tomato; sprinkle with basil and vinegar. Serve with salad greens, if desired.

serves 4
per serving 30.3g fat (7.3g saturated); 2454kJ (587 cal); 31.6g carb

vegetable frittata

A frittata is the Italian version of a filled omelette, the main difference being that it is oven-baked while an omelette is cooked on top of the stove.

2 medium potatoes (400g), peeled, cut into 1cm slices
1 medium kumara (400g), peeled, cut into 1cm slices
10 eggs
½ cup (125ml) cream
1 cup (80g) coarsely grated parmesan cheese
½ cup (60g) coarsely grated cheddar cheese
50g baby rocket leaves
2 tablespoons finely shredded fresh basil

1 Preheat oven to moderate. Oil and line deep 19cm-square cake pan.
2 Boil, steam or microwave potato and kumara, separately, until just tender; drain.
3 Meanwhile, whisk eggs, cream and cheeses in large jug.
4 Layer potato slices in cake pan; top with rocket, then kumara slices, then basil. Carefully pour egg mixture over vegetables in pan.
5 Bake frittata, covered, in moderate oven 45 minutes. Remove from oven; stand frittata in pan for 5 minutes before slicing into triangles.

serves 4
per serving 38.6g fat (20.4g saturated);
2412kJ (577 cal); 25.4g carb
tips You can replace the rocket with baby spinach leaves. To reduce the fat content of the frittata, replace the cream with low-fat milk.

tuna salad bruschetta

425g can tuna chunks in springwater, drained
⅓ cup (100g) mayonnaise
1 medium red onion (170g), chopped finely
⅓ cup coarsely chopped fresh flat-leaf parsley
1 loaf ciabatta, cut into 8 slices

1 Combine tuna, mayonnaise, onion and parsley in medium bowl.
2 Toast ciabatta; divide tuna salad between slices.

serves 4
per serving 15.3g fat (2.4g saturated); 2475kJ (592 cal); 80g carb

onion and anchovy tartlets

1 tablespoon olive oil
60g butter
3 medium brown onions (450g), halved, sliced thinly
2 cloves garlic, crushed
1 bay leaf
3 sprigs fresh thyme
⅓ cup coarsely chopped fresh flat-leaf parsley
8 anchovy fillets, drained, chopped finely
2 tablespoons coarsely chopped seeded kalamata olives
¾ cup (110q) self-raising flour
¾ cup (110g) plain flour
¾ cup (180ml) buttermilk

1 Heat oil and half of the butter in large frying pan;
cook onion, garlic, bay leaf and thyme, stirring occasionally,
about 20 minutes or until onion caramelises. Discard
bay leaf and thyme; stir in parsley, anchovy and olives.
2 Meanwhile, blend or process flours and remaining butter
until mixture resembles fine breadcrumbs. Add buttermilk;
process until ingredients just come together. Knead
dough on lightly floured surface until smooth.
3 Preheat oven to moderately hot. Oil two oven trays.
4 Divide dough into six pieces; roll each piece of dough
on floured surface into 14cm square. Fold edges over
to form 1cm border.
5 Place squares on prepared trays; spread rounded
tablespoons of the onion mixture on each square.
Bake, uncovered, in moderately hot oven about
15 minutes or until pastry browns lightly.

serves 6
per serving 12.9g fat (6.4g saturated);
1150kJ (275 cal); 31.8g carb

antipasto puff pastry tartlets

¼ cup (60ml) olive oil
2 cloves garlic, crushed
1 small red capsicum (150g), chopped coarsely
1 small yellow capsicum (150g), chopped coarsely
1 medium zucchini (120g), sliced thinly
2 baby eggplants (120g), sliced thinly
1 small red onion (100g), sliced thickly
100g semi-dried tomatoes
150g cherry bocconcini, halved
½ cup (40g) finely grated parmesan cheese
½ cup firmly packed fresh basil leaves
2 sheets ready-rolled puff pastry
⅓ cup (85g) bottled tomato pasta sauce
2 tablespoons bottled olive tapenade

1 Preheat oven to moderately hot.
2 Combine oil and garlic in large bowl. Add capsicums, zucchini, eggplant and onion; toss gently to coat vegetables in mixture.
3 Cook vegetables, in batches, on heated oiled grill plate (or grill or barbecue) until browned lightly and just tender; transfer to large bowl. Add tomatoes, cheeses and basil; toss gently to combine.
4 Cut pastry sheets in half; fold edges 1cm inward, place on oiled oven trays. Divide sauce among pastry pieces; top with vegetable mixture. Bake, uncovered, in moderately hot oven about 15 minutes or until browned lightly. Serve tartlets topped with tapenade.

serves 4
per serving 43.3g fat (18.1g saturated); 2750kJ (658 cal); 47.2g carb

lamb kofta platter

650g lamb mince
1 medium brown onion (150g), chopped finely
1 clove garlic, crushed
1 teaspoon ground cumin
1 teaspoon ground coriander
1 cup (70g) stale breadcrumbs
1 egg, beaten lightly
4 pocket pitta
1 tablespoon olive oil
200g tabbouleh
1 medium tomato (150g), chopped finely
200g hummus
1 teaspoon olive oil, extra
¼ teaspoon sweet paprika
200g beetroot dip
1 medium lemon (140g), cut into wedges

1 Combine lamb, onion, garlic, spices, breadcrumbs and egg in medium bowl.
2 Shape mixture into 12 ovals and thread onto skewers. Cook the skewers on heated oiled grill plate (or grill or barbecue) until browned and cooked through.
3 Brush bread with oil, cook on heated grill plate until browned.
4 Combine tabbouleh and tomato in medium bowl. Drizzle hummus with extra oil, sprinkle with paprika.
5 Serve kofta skewers with bread, tabbouleh, hummus, beetroot dip and lemon wedges.

serves 4
per serving 38.3g fat (9.7g saturated); 3507kJ (839 cal); 70g carb
tips This recipe can be prepared several hours ahead. You will need to soak 12 bamboo skewers in water for at least an hour before use to prevent them from scorching.

fajitas with salsa cruda and avocado mash

2 tablespoons vegetable oil
⅓ cup (80ml) lime juice
¼ cup coarsely chopped
  fresh oregano
2 cloves garlic, crushed
¼ cup coarsely chopped
  fresh coriander
2 teaspoons ground cumin
800g beef skirt steak
1 medium red capsicum (200g),
  sliced thickly
1 medium green capsicum (200g),
  sliced thickly
1 medium yellow capsicum (200g),
  sliced thickly
1 large red onion (300g), sliced thickly
20 small flour tortillas
salsa cruda
2 cloves garlic, crushed
3 medium tomatoes (450g), seeded,
  chopped finely
1 small white onion (80g),
  chopped finely
2 trimmed red radishes (30g),
  chopped finely
1 lebanese cucumber (130g),
  chopped finely
2 tablespoons coarsely chopped
  fresh coriander
1 fresh long red chilli, chopped finely
2 tablespoons lime juice
avocado mash
2 small avocados (400g)
2 tablespoons lime juice

1 Combine oil, juice, oregano, garlic, coriander and cumin in large bowl, add beef; toss beef to coat in marinade. Cover; refrigerate 3 hours or overnight.
2 Cook beef, capsicums and onion on heated oiled flat plate, uncovered, until beef is cooked as desired and vegetables are just tender. Cover to keep warm.
3 Meanwhile, make salsa cruda and avocado mash. Warm tortillas according to directions on packet.
4 Cut beef into 1cm slices; combine with cooked vegetables in large bowl. Serve with salsa cruda, avocado mash and tortillas.
salsa cruda Combine ingredients in small bowl.
avocado mash Mash avocado and juice in small bowl.

serves 4
per serving 46.7g fat (9.1g saturated); 5229kJ (1251 cal); 134g carb

pork and corn salsa tortilla wraps

600g pork fillet, sliced thinly
2 tablespoons vegetable oil
35g packet Taco Seasoning Mix
16 small corn tortillas
310g can corn kernels, drained
3 medium tomatoes (450g), chopped coarsely
1 small red onion (100g), chopped finely
¼ cup coarsely chopped fresh coriander
1 butter lettuce, torn
½ cup (120g) light sour cream

1 Combine pork, oil and taco seasoning mix in medium bowl.
2 Warm the tortillas according to directions on packet.
3 Cook pork on heated oiled grill plate or in large frying pan until pork is browned and cooked through.
4 Combine corn, tomato, onion and coriander in medium bowl.
5 Serve pork wrapped in tortillas with corn salsa, lettuce and sour cream.

serves 4
per serving 23.9g fat (6.9g saturated);
3265kJ (781 cal); 92g carb
tip This recipe can be prepared several hours ahead; cook and assemble just before serving.

gourmet chicken sandwiches

Black cumin seeds, also sold as jeera kala, are darker and sweeter than ordinary cumin and are sometimes confused with kalonji (nigella seeds). Used extensively in Indian and Moroccan-style cooking, the nutty flavour of black cumin seeds is brought out by toasting.

600g chicken breast fillets
2 cups (500ml) chicken stock
1½ cups (375ml) water
⅓ cup (50g) drained
   sun-dried tomatoes
1 tablespoon coarsely chopped
   fresh rosemary
2 tablespoons chicken
   stock, extra
½ loaf turkish bread (215g)
½ small red onion (50g),
   sliced thinly
1 lebanese cucumber (130g),
   sliced thinly
60g baby rocket leaves
⅓ cup (95g) yogurt
½ teaspoon toasted black
   cumin seeds

1 Combine chicken, stock and the water in large saucepan; bring to a boil. Reduce heat; simmer, uncovered, about 10 minutes or until cooked through. Cool chicken in poaching liquid 10 minutes. Remove chicken from pan; discard poaching liquid (or reserve for another use). Slice chicken thinly.

2 Meanwhile, drain tomatoes on absorbent paper, pressing firmly to remove as much oil as possible. Quarter tomatoes; blend or process with rosemary and extra stock until tomato mixture forms a paste.

3 Halve turkish bread, slice pieces horizontally; toast both sides. Spread cut sides of bread with tomato paste; top with chicken, onion, cucumber and rocket. Serve with combined yogurt and seeds.

serves 4
per serving 7.3g fat (2g saturated); 1559kJ (373 cal); 32.2g carb

lamb patties with beetroot and tzatziki

500g lamb mince
1 small brown onion (80g), chopped finely
1 medium carrot (120g), grated coarsely
1 egg, beaten lightly
2 tablespoons finely chopped fresh flat-leaf parsley
1 teaspoon finely grated lemon rind
½ teaspoon dried oregano leaves
2 cloves garlic, crushed
½ cup (140g) yogurt
1 lebanese cucumber (130g), seeded, chopped finely
1 tablespoon finely chopped fresh mint
1 loaf turkish bread (430g)
1 cup (60g) coarsely shredded cos lettuce
225g can sliced beetroot, drained
1 medium lemon (140g), cut into wedges

1 Using hands, combine lamb, onion, carrot,
egg, parsley, rind, oregano and half of the garlic
in medium bowl; shape lamb mixture into four patties.
Cook patties on heated oiled grill plate (or grill or barbecue)
until cooked through.
2 Meanwhile, combine yogurt, cucumber, mint and
remaining garlic in small bowl. Cut bread into four pieces;
split each piece in half horizontally. Toast bread cut-side up.
3 Sandwich lettuce, patties, yogurt mixture and beetroot
between bread pieces. Serve with lemon wedges.

serves 4
per serving 14.9g fat (5.6g saturated);
2207kJ (528 cal); 56.9g carb

the best beer-battered fish and chips

1kg potatoes, peeled
peanut oil, for deep-frying
1⅔ cups (250g) self-raising flour
1 cup (250ml) beer (or soda water)
1 cup (250ml) cold water
8 skinless flathead fillets (960g)

1 Preheat oven to moderately slow.
2 Cut potatoes lengthways into 1cm slices; cut each slice lengthways into 1cm-wide pieces. Stand potato pieces in large bowl of cold water for 30 minutes to avoid discolouration. Drain; pat dry with a clean tea towel.
3 Heat oil in a deep-fryer, wok or large saucepan to 180°C; cook chips in batches for about 4 minutes each batch, or until just tender but not browned. Drain well on absorbent paper.
4 Reheat oil, cook chips, in batches, separating any that stick together by shaking deep-fryer basket or with a slotted spoon, until crisp and golden brown. Drain on absorbent paper; spread out on an oven tray; keep hot in a moderately slow oven.
5 Whisk flour, beer and the water together in medium bowl until smooth.
6 Reheat oil. Dip fish in batter and deep-fry in hot oil until browned, crisp and just cooked through. Drain well on absorbent paper.
7 Serve fish immediately with chips, sprinkled with salt and with lemon wedges, if desired.

serves 4
per serving 15.4g fat (3.3g saturated); 2955kJ (707 cal); 74g carb
tip This recipe is best made close to serving. The chips can be fried until tender several hours ahead.

seafood skewers with radicchio and fennel salad

Any firm white fish fillet, such as blue-eye or ling, can be used in this recipe.

8 uncooked large king
　prawns (560g)
8 cleaned baby octopus (720g)
400g firm white fish fillets
8 scallops (200g), roe removed
2 teaspoons fennel seeds
2 teaspoons dried green
　peppercorns
2 tablespoons white wine vinegar
2 cloves garlic, crushed
1 tablespoon olive oil
2 medium radicchio (400g)
2 small fennel bulbs (400g),
　trimmed, sliced thinly
1 cup firmly packed fresh
　flat-leaf parsley leaves
mustard dressing
¼ cup (60ml) white wine vinegar
½ teaspoon mustard powder
1 tablespoon olive oil
1 teaspoon sugar
4 green onions, chopped coarsely

1 Shell and devein prawns, leaving tails intact. Remove heads and beaks from octopus. Cut fish into 2.5cm pieces. Combine seafood in large bowl.
2 Using mortar and pestle, crush seeds and peppercorns coarsely, add to seafood with vinegar, garlic and oil; toss gently to combine. Cover; refrigerate 3 hours or overnight.
3 Make mustard dressing.
4 Thread seafood, alternating varieties, on skewers; cook on heated lightly oiled grill plate (or grill or barbecue) until seafood is just changed in colour and cooked as desired.
5 Meanwhile, discard dark outer leaves of radicchio, tear inner leaves roughly. Combine radicchio in medium bowl with fennel, parsley and dressing; toss gently to combine. Serve seafood skewers on salad.
mustard dressing Place ingredients in screw-top jar; shake well.

serves 4
per serving 13.9g fat (2.2g saturated); 2082kJ (498 cal); 6.6g carb
tips Use green peppercorns in brine if you can't find the dried variety; rinse then drain them thoroughly before using.
You will need to soak eight bamboo skewers in water for at least an hour before use to prevent splintering and scorching.

moroccan blue-eye kebabs with almond and lemon couscous

½ cup finely chopped fresh coriander
2 cloves garlic, crushed
2 tablespoons olive oil
2 fresh small red thai chillies, chopped finely
¼ cup (60ml) lemon juice
800g skinless blue-eye fillets, diced into 3cm pieces
1½ cups (375ml) chicken stock
1½ cups (300g) couscous
½ cup firmly packed fresh coriander leaves
1 tablespoon finely chopped preserved lemon
¼ cup (35g) toasted slivered almonds

1 Combine chopped coriander, garlic, oil, chilli and juice in small bowl. Place half of the coriander mixture in large bowl, add fish; toss fish to coat in mixture. Thread fish onto skewers; place kebabs on tray. Cover; refrigerate 45 minutes.

2 Cook kebabs on heated lightly oiled grill plate (or grill or barbecue) about 5 minutes or until cooked as desired.

3 Meanwhile, bring stock to a boil in small saucepan; remove from heat. Add couscous to stock, cover; stand about 5 minutes or until liquid is absorbed, fluffing with fork occasionally. Add remaining coriander mixture, coriander leaves, lemon and nuts; toss gently to combine. Serve couscous with kebabs.

serves 4
per serving 16.2g fat (2.1g saturated);
2424kJ (580 cal); 59.4g carb
tip You will need to soak eight bamboo skewers in water for at least an hour before use to prevent them from splintering or scorching.

grilled lamb cutlets with warm risoni salad

Risoni is a small rice-shaped pasta very similar to orzo; you can use either for this recipe.

1 clove garlic, crushed
1 tablespoon finely chopped
   fresh oregano
1 tablespoon finely chopped
   fresh chives
2 tablespoons lemon juice
¼ cup (60ml) dry white wine
12 french-trimmed lamb
   cutlets (700g)
warm risoni salad
500g pumpkin, cut into
   3cm pieces
1 clove garlic, crushed
1 tablespoon olive oil
1 cup (220g) risoni
150g baby spinach leaves
2 tablespoons lemon juice
2 tablespoons coarsely
   chopped fresh chives
2 tablespoons fresh
   oregano leaves

1 Combine garlic, oregano, chives, juice and wine in large bowl, add lamb; toss lamb to coat in marinade. Cover; refrigerate 3 hours or overnight.
2 Meanwhile, make warm risoni salad.
3 Drain lamb; discard marinade. Cook lamb, in batches, on heated lightly oiled grill plate (or grill or barbecue) until cooked as desired. Serve lamb with salad.

warm risoni salad Preheat oven to moderately hot. Place pumpkin, in single layer, on oven tray; drizzle with combined garlic and half of the oil. Roast, uncovered, in moderately hot oven about 15 minutes or until pumpkin is browned lightly and tender. Meanwhile, cook pasta in large saucepan of boiling water, uncovered, until just tender; drain. Combine pasta and spinach in large bowl with pumpkin, juice, herbs and remaining oil; toss gently to combine.

serves 4
per serving 20.7g fat (7.9g saturated); 2040kJ (488 cal); 45.1g carb

chicken wings and green mango salad

10cm stick (20g) fresh
  lemon grass, chopped finely
1 fresh long green chilli,
  chopped finely
3 cloves garlic, crushed
10 fresh kaffir lime leaves,
  shredded finely
16 chicken wings (1.5kg)
2 small green mangoes (600g)
1 large carrot (180g)
1 lebanese cucumber (130g)
1 medium red capsicum
  (200g), sliced thinly
2 green onions, sliced thinly
sweet and sour dressing
2 tablespoons fish sauce
2 tablespoons lime juice
2 tablespoons grated
  palm sugar
1 tablespoon white vinegar
1 tablespoon water

1 Make sweet and sour dressing.

2 Combine lemon grass, chilli, garlic, half of the lime leaves and 2 tablespoons of the dressing in medium bowl, add chicken; toss chicken to coat in marinade. Cover remaining dressing and chicken separately; refrigerate 3 hours or overnight.

3 Drain chicken; discard marinade. Cook chicken on heated oiled grill plate, uncovered, until cooked through.

4 Meanwhile, use vegetable peeler to finely slice mangoes, carrot and cucumber into ribbons. Place in medium bowl with capsicum, remaining lime leaves and remaining dressing; toss gently to combine. Serve chicken with salad, sprinkled with onion.

sweet and sour dressing Place ingredients in screw-top jar; shake well.

serves 4
per serving 13g fat (4.1g saturated); 1877kJ (449 cal); 25.2g carb

cajun chicken with chunky salsa

4 single chicken breast fillets (680g)
1 teaspoon cracked black pepper
2 tablespoons finely chopped fresh oregano
2 teaspoons sweet paprika
1 teaspoon dried chilli flakes
2 cloves garlic, crushed
2 teaspoons olive oil
chunky salsa
2 medium tomatoes (300g), chopped coarsely
1 small red onion (100g), chopped coarsely
1 medium green capsicum (200g), chopped coarsely
2 tablespoons coarsely chopped fresh coriander
2 teaspoons olive oil
2 tablespoons lime juice

1 Place chicken in large bowl with combined remaining ingredients; toss chicken to coat in mixture. Cover; refrigerate 15 minutes.
2 Meanwhile, make chunky salsa.
3 Cook chicken in large lightly oiled non-stick frying pan until cooked through. Serve chicken with salsa.
chunky salsa Combine ingredients in medium bowl.

serves 4
per serving 8.7g fat (1.7g saturated); 1083kJ (259 cal); 4.1g carb
tip Serve with warm corn tortillas, if desired.

spicy chicken legs with mango salad

2 teaspoons sesame oil
8 chicken drumsticks (1.2kg)
½ cup (125ml) chicken stock
2 teaspoons honey
2 tablespoons rice vinegar
1 teaspoon five-spice powder
6 cloves garlic, crushed
¼ cup (60ml) soy sauce
½ cup (125ml) water
mango salad
1 green mango (350g),
    sliced thinly
4 green onions, sliced thinly
1 cup loosely packed
    coriander leaves
150g snow peas,
    trimmed, halved
2 lebanese cucumbers (260g),
    seeded, sliced thinly
1½ cups (120g) bean sprouts
lime and vinegar dressing
¼ cup (60ml) lime juice
¼ cup (60ml) rice vinegar
2 teaspoons peanut oil

1 Heat oil in large deep frying pan; cook chicken, in batches, about 5 minutes or until browned all over.
2 Meanwhile, combine remaining ingredients in medium jug.
3 Return chicken to pan with stock mixture; bring to a boil. Reduce heat; simmer, covered, about 20 minutes or until chicken is cooked through.
4 Meanwhile, make mango salad and lime and vinegar dressing.
5 Pour dressing onto salad; toss gently to combine. Divide chicken and salad among serving plates; drizzle remaining pan juices over chicken.
mango salad Combine ingredients in large bowl.
lime and vinegar dressing Place ingredients in screw-top jar; shake well.

serves 4
per serving 26.1g fat (7.2g saturated); 1914kJ (458 cal); 16.3g carb

marjoram and lemon veal chops with greek salad

1 teaspoon finely grated
  lemon rind
¼ cup (60ml) lemon juice
1 tablespoon finely chopped
  fresh marjoram
2 teaspoons olive oil
4 x 200g veal chops
greek salad
¾ cup (120g) seeded
  kalamata olives
200g fetta cheese,
  chopped coarsely
6 large egg tomatoes (540g),
  seeded, chopped coarsely
1 medium red capsicum (200g),
  chopped coarsely
2 lebanese cucumbers (260g),
  seeded, sliced thinly
2 trimmed celery stalks (200g),
  sliced thinly
1 tablespoon fresh
  marjoram leaves
lemon dressing
1 clove garlic, crushed
⅓ cup (80ml) lemon juice
2 teaspoons olive oil

1 Combine rind, juice, marjoram and oil in large bowl, add veal; toss veal to coat in marinade. Cover; refrigerate 1 hour.
2 Meanwhile, make greek salad and lemon dressing.
3 Cook veal on heated lightly oiled grill plate (or grill or barbeque) until cooked as desired.
4 Pour dressing over salad; toss gently to combine. Serve veal with salad.
greek salad Combine ingredients in large bowl.
lemon dressing Place ingredients in screw-top jar; shake well.

serves 4
per serving 19.9g fat (9.3g saturated); 1705kJ (408 cal); 15g carb

basil and oregano steak with char-grilled vegetables

2 teaspoons finely chopped fresh oregano
¼ cup finely chopped fresh basil
1 tablespoon finely grated lemon rind
2 tablespoons lemon juice
4 drained anchovy fillets, chopped finely
4 x 200g beef sirloin steaks
2 baby fennel bulbs (260g), quartered
3 small zucchini (270g), chopped coarsely
1 large red capsicum (350g), sliced thickly
200g portobello mushrooms, sliced thickly
4 baby eggplants (240g), chopped coarsely
2 small red onions (200g), sliced thickly
2 teaspoons olive oil
¼ cup (60ml) lemon juice, extra
2 tablespoons fresh oregano leaves

1 Combine chopped oregano, basil, rind, the 2 tablespoons of lemon juice and anchovy in large bowl, add beef; toss beef to coat in marinade. Cover; refrigerate 3 hours or overnight.
2 Meanwhile, combine fennel, zucchini, capsicum, mushroom, eggplant, onion and oil in large bowl; cook vegetables, in batches, on heated lightly oiled grill plate (or grill or barbecue) until just tender. Add extra juice and oregano leaves to bowl with vegetables; toss gently to combine. Cover to keep warm.
3 Cook beef mixture on same grill plate until cooked as desired; serve with vegetables.

serves 4
per serving 21.7g fat (8.6g saturated);
1823kJ (436 cal); 11g carb

pork steaks with beetroot salad

300g baby beetroot
1 tablespoon caraway seeds
2 teaspoons olive oil
4 x 175g butterflied pork steaks
150g firm goat cheese, crumbled
5 large red radishes (175g), trimmed, sliced thinly
125g baby rocket leaves
dijon vinaigrette
2 teaspoons dijon mustard
2 teaspoons olive oil
2 tablespoons red wine vinegar

1 Preheat oven to moderately hot.
2 Discard beetroot stems and leaves; place unpeeled beetroot in small shallow baking dish. Roast, uncovered, in moderately hot oven about 45 minutes or until beetroot is tender. Cool 10 minutes; peel, cut into quarters.
3 Meanwhile, make dijon vinaigrette.
4 Using mortar and pestle, crush seeds and oil into smooth paste; rub into pork. Cook pork on heated lightly oiled grill plate (or grill or barbecue) until cooked as desired.
5 Place beetroot and vinaigrette in large bowl with cheese, radish and rocket; toss gently to combine. Serve pork with salad.
dijon vinaigrette Place ingredients in screw-top jar; shake well.

serves 4
per serving 23.5g fat (8.7g saturated); 1818kJ (435 cal); 8.3g carb

chicken sang choy bow

You need about two medium butter lettuce for this recipe.

4 dried shiitake mushrooms
1 tablespoon peanut oil
1kg chicken mince
4cm piece fresh ginger (20g), chopped finely
1 clove garlic, crushed
227g can water chestnuts, drained, chopped coarsely
227g can sliced bamboo shoots, drained,
  chopped coarsely
¼ cup (60ml) hoisin sauce
¼ cup (60ml) oyster sauce
2 tablespoons soy sauce
2 tablespoons cornflour
½ cup (125ml) chicken stock
3 cups (240g) bean sprouts
4 green onions, sliced thickly
18 large butter lettuce leaves

1 Place mushrooms in small heatproof bowl, cover with boiling water; stand 20 minutes, drain. Discard stems; chop mushroom caps finely.
2 Heat oil in wok; stir-fry chicken, ginger and garlic until chicken is just changed in colour.
3 Add mushrooms with water chestnuts, bamboo shoots, sauces and blended cornflour and stock; stir-fry until mixture boils and thickens. Stir in sprouts and onion.
4 Divide lettuce leaves among serving plates; spoon sang choy bow into lettuce leaves.

serves 6
per serving 17.8g fat (4.7g saturated); 1534kJ (367 cal); 15.8g carb

tex-mex spareribs with grilled corn salsa

2 tablespoons brown sugar
1 tablespoon dried oregano
2 tablespoons sweet paprika
2 teaspoons cracked black pepper
½ teaspoon cayenne pepper
1 tablespoon ground cumin
1 tablespoon garlic powder
¼ cup (60ml) water
2 tablespoons vegetable oil
1.5kg American-style pork spareribs
3 trimmed corn cobs (750g)
2 medium tomatoes (300g), seeded, chopped finely
1 fresh long green chilli, chopped finely
1 medium red onion (170g), chopped finely
1 medium green capsicum (200g), chopped finely
¼ cup coarsely chopped fresh coriander
2 tablespoons lime juice
1 tablespoon olive oil

1 Combine sugar, oregano, spices, the water and oil in large bowl; add pork, rub spice mixture all over pork. Cook pork on heated oiled flat plate, uncovered, until cooked as desired.
2 Meanwhile, cook corn on heated oiled grill plate, uncovered, until tender. When cool enough to handle, cut kernels from cobs. Place kernels in medium bowl with remaining ingredients; toss salsa gently to combine. Serve with pork.

serves 4
per serving 33.7g fat (9.1g saturated); 2445kJ (585 cal); 33.9g carb

fresh prawn spring rolls

125g vermicelli noodles
2 tablespoons lime juice
2 tablespoons palm sugar
1 tablespoon fish sauce
1 lebanese cucumber (130g), seeded
16 x 16cm-round rice paper sheets
16 large fresh mint leaves
16 medium cooked prawns, shelled
8 green onions, sliced thinly
16 sprigs fresh coriander
1 cup (50g) snow pea sprouts
dipping sauce
½ cup (125ml) sweet chilli sauce
2 tablespoon lime juice

1 Place vermicelli noodles in medium bowl of hot water
for 5 minutes or until softened; drain well. Chop the
noodles coarsely.
2 Combine noodles with lime juice, sugar and fish sauce
in medium bowl. Cut cucumber into thin strips.
3 Cover a board with a damp tea towel. Place 1 sheet
of rice paper in bowl of warm water until softened.
Place on tea towel, top with a mint leaf, prawn and
1 heaped tablespoon of the noodle mixture, cucumber,
green onions, coriander and sprouts. Fold sides and
roll up to enclose.
4 Repeat with remaining rice paper sheets and
remaining ingredients. Place rolls on a tray lined
with plastic wrap; cover with damp paper towel
and refrigerate until ready to serve.
dipping sauce Combine sauce and juice in small bowl.

serves 4
per serving 2.5g fat (0.5g saturated);
1421kJ (340 cal); 51.4g carb

zucchini fritters with tzatziki

4 medium zucchini (480g), grated coarsely
1 teaspoon salt
1 medium brown onion (150g), chopped finely
¾ cup (50g) stale breadcrumbs
2 eggs, beaten lightly
1 tablespoon finely chopped fresh oregano
1 tablespoon finely chopped fresh mint
2 tablespoons extra virgin olive oil
tzatziki
2 cups (560g) thick Greek-style yogurt
1 lebanese cucumber (130g)
1 clove garlic, crushed
2 tablespoons finely chopped fresh mint
2 tablespoons lemon juice
½ teaspoon sea salt

1 Combine zucchini and salt, toss. Stand 15 minutes then squeeze out excess liquid. Combine with onion, breadcrumbs, egg, oregano and mint.
2 Preheat oven to very slow.
3 Heat oil in non-stick frying pan over medium heat; drop in level tablespoons of zucchini mixture, flatten slightly; cook until browned on both sides and cooked through. Transfer to an oven tray; place in oven to keep warm. Repeat with remaining mixture.
4 Serve fritters with tzatziki.
tzatziki Line a sieve with absorbent paper, add yogurt; place sieve over medium bowl. Cover; refrigerate 4 hours. Halve cucumber lengthways; remove seeds. Coarsely grate flesh and skin. Squeeze out excess liquid. Combine yogurt, cucumber, garlic, mint, juice and salt in medium bowl.

serves 8 as a starter
per serving 11.2g fat (4.3g saturated);
765kJ (183 cal); 12.7g carb

potato and rosemary pizza

2 teaspoons (7g) dry yeast
½ teaspoon caster sugar
¾ cup (180ml) warm water
2 cups (300g) plain flour
1 teaspoon salt
2 tablespoons olive oil
2 tablespoons polenta
4 small potatoes (100g),
  sliced thinly
2 tablespoons fresh rosemary
2 cloves garlic, crushed
1 tablespoon olive oil, extra

1 Combine yeast, sugar and the water in small bowl; cover, stand in warm place about 10 minutes or until frothy.

2 Sift flour and salt into large bowl. Stir in yeast mixture and olive oil; mix to soft dough. Bring dough together with your hands and add a little extra water if necessary.

3 Knead dough on lightly floured surface for 10 minutes or until smooth and elastic. Push dough with heel of your hand and give it a quarter turn each time. Place dough in lightly oiled large bowl; cover, stand in warm place about 1 hour or until doubled in size.

4 Preheat oven to very hot. Punch dough down with fist, then knead on lightly floured surface until smooth. Divide dough in half. Roll each half to a 20cm x 35cm rectangle, then place on oiled rectangular trays sprinkled with polenta. Prick bases with fork.

5 Layer potatoes, overlapping slightly, over top of pizza. Sprinkle with rosemary; drizzle with combined garlic and extra oil.

6 Bake on lowest shelf in very hot oven about 15 minutes or until base and potato are browned and crisp. Sprinkle with salt before serving.

makes 2 thin pizzas
per pizza 29.8g fat (4.2g saturated); 3908kJ (935 cal); 142g carb

tips This recipe is best made close to serving. The dough can be made in a breadmaker, following the manufacturer's instructions.

pineapple and mint ice-blocks

lemonade ice-bl

raspberry ice-blocks

orange and mango ice-b

pineapple and mint ice-blocks

Combine 1½ cups (375ml) pineapple juice, 2 tablespoons icing sugar mixture and 2 teaspoons finely chopped fresh mint in medium jug. Pour mixture into six ¼-cup (60ml) ice-block moulds. Press lids on firmly; freeze overnight.

makes 6
per block 0.1g fat (0g saturated); 184kJ (44 cal); 10.6g carb

raspberry ice-blocks

Heat 1 cup (150g) frozen raspberries and ⅓ cup (55g) icing sugar mixture in small saucepan over low heat, stirring occasionally, about 5 minutes or until raspberries soften. Using back of large spoon, push raspberry mixture through sieve into medium jug; discard seeds. Stir 1 cup (250ml) sparkling mineral water into jug. Pour mixture into six ¼-cup (60ml) ice-block moulds. Press lids on firmly; freeze overnight.

makes 6
per block 0.1g fat (0g saturated); 184kJ (44 cal); 10.6g carb

lemonade ice-blocks

Stir ¼ cup (60ml) lemon juice and ⅔ cup (110g) icing sugar mixture in medium jug until sugar dissolves. Stir in 1 cup (250ml) sparkling mineral water. Pour mixture into six ¼-cup (60ml) ice-block moulds. Press lids on firmly; freeze overnight.

makes 6
per block 0g fat; 305kJ (73 cal); 18.5g carb

orange and mango ice-blocks

Strain 425g can sliced mango in natural juice over small bowl; reserve juice. Blend or process mango slices, ¼ cup (60ml) of the reserved juice and ½ cup (125ml) orange juice until smooth. Pour mixture into six ¼-cup (60ml) ice-block moulds. Press lids on firmly; freeze overnight.

makes 6
per block 0.1g fat (0g saturated); 188kJ (45 cal); 10.3g carb

glossary

bamboo shoots tender shoots of bamboo plants, available in cans; drain/rinse before use.

basil, thai also called horapa; different from sweet basil. Having smaller leaves and purplish stems, it has a slight licorice or aniseed taste.

bean sprouts also known as bean shoots; new growths of assorted beans and seeds.

breadcrumbs, stale one- or two-day-old bread crumbed by grating, blending or processing.

butter use salted or unsalted "sweet" butter; 125g is equal to 1 stick butter.

buttermilk sold in refrigerated section in supermarkets. Originally, the liquid left after cream was separated from milk; today, it is commercially made similarly to yogurt.

capsicum also known as bell pepper or, simply, pepper.

cayenne pepper long, very hot red chilli usually sold dried and ground.

cheese

bocconcini: walnut-sized, baby mozzarella, a delicate, semi-soft, white cheese. Must be kept in refrigerator, in brine, for one or two days at most.

cheddar: common cow-milk "tasty" cheese; should be aged and hard with a bite.

fetta: crumbly goat- or sheep-milk cheese with a salty taste.

goat: made from goat milk, has a strong, earthy taste; available in both soft and firm textures.

parmesan: also known as parmigiano; hard, grainy cow-milk cheese, originally from Parma in Italy, that is aged for up to two years.

chilli use rubber gloves when seeding/chopping fresh chilli to prevent burning your skin.

dried flakes: dehydrated fine slices and whole seeds.

red thai: also known as "scuds"; small, medium-hot, and bright red in colour.

ciabatta popular Italian wood-fired white bread.

coriander also called cilantro or chinese parsley; leafy, bright-green herb. Also sold as seeds, whole or ground.

cornflour also known as cornstarch; used to thicken.

cos lettuce also known as romaine lettuce.

couscous fine, grain-like cereal product, made from semolina.

cumin also known as zeera; dried seeds having a spicy, nutty flavour. Available as seeds or in ground form.

eggplant vegetable with purple skin; also known as aubergine.

fennel bulb vegetable, also known as finocchio or anise. Also the name given to dried seeds having a licorice flavour.

fish sauce made from salted, fermented fish; has a pungent smell and a strong taste.

five-spice powder a fragrant mixture of ground cinnamon, cloves, star anise, sichuan pepper and fennel seeds.

flour

plain: an all-purpose flour, made from wheat.

self-raising: plain flour sifted with baking powder in the proportion of 1 cup flour to 2 teaspoons baking powder.

ginger also known as green or root ginger; the thick gnarled root of a tropical plant.

green peppercorns soft, unripe berry of pepper plant, usually sold packed in brine.

hoisin sauce thick, sweet and spicy Chinese paste made from salted fermented soy beans.

kaffir lime leaves also known as bai magrood; two glossy dark-green leaves joined end to end, forming a rounded hourglass shape, from the kaffir lime tree. Available fresh or dried; replace with a strip of fresh lime peel, if necessary.

kumara Polynesian name of orange-fleshed sweet potato.

lebanese cucumber long, slender and thin-skinned; also known as the european or burpless cucumber.

lemon grass a tall, clumping, lemon-smelling and tasting, sharp-edged grass; the white lower part of the stem is used.

mayonnaise we use whole-egg mayonnaise in our recipes.

mince meat also known as ground meat.

mint, vietnamese a pungent, peppery narrow-leafed member of the buckwheat family. Also known as cambodian mint or laksa leaf.

mizuna Japanese in origin; frizzy, green salad leaf having a delicate mustard flavour.

mushroom

portobello: large, dark-brown mushrooms possessing a full-bodied flavour.

shiitake: when fresh, are also known as chinese black, forest or golden oak mushrooms; have earthy taste. When dried, they are known as donko or dried chinese mushrooms; rehydrate before use.

mustard

powder: finely ground white (yellow) mustard seeds.

dijon: pale, mild French mustard with distinctive flavour.

oil

peanut: pressed from ground peanuts; most commonly used oil in Asian cooking because of its high smoke point (capacity to handle high heat without burning).

sesame: made from roasted, crushed, white sesame seeds; a flavouring rather than a cooking medium.

olive tapenade a thick, black paste made of olives, olive oil, capers, anchovies and herbs.

onion

green: also known as scallion or (incorrectly) shallot; an immature onion picked before the bulb has formed, having a long, bright-green edible stalk.

red: also known as spanish, red spanish or bermuda onion; a sweet-flavoured, large, purple-red onion.

oyster sauce rich, brown sauce made from oysters and their brine, salt and soy sauce.

paprika ground dried red capsicum, available sweet, hot or smoked.

parsley, flat-leaf also known as continental or italian parsley.

pocket pitta wheat-flour bread sold in small, flat pieces that separate into two thin rounds.

polenta also called cornmeal; a cereal of dried corn (maize), sold ground in different textures.

prawns also known as shrimp.

preserved lemon preserved in salt, olive oil and lemon juice, these lemons impart a rich,

salty-sour acidic flavour; rinse preserved lemon well under cold water before using.

pumpkin also called squash.

radicchio has dark burgundy leaves and strong, bitter taste.

rice paper sheets also known as banh trang. Made from rice paste and stamped into rounds; dipped briefly in water, they become pliable wrappers.

risoni small rice-shaped pasta.

rocket also known as arugula, rugula and rucola; a peppery-tasting green leaf.

snow peas also known as mange tout ("eat all").

soy sauce also known as sieu; made from fermented soy beans.

spinach also known as english spinach and, incorrectly, silverbeet.

star anise dried, star-shaped pod that imparts an astringent, aniseed flavour.

sugar

brown: soft, fine granulated sugar retaining molasses.

caster: also called superfine or finely granulated table sugar.

icing sugar mixture: also known as confectioners' sugar or powdered sugar; pulverised, granulated sugar crushed with a small amount (about 3%) cornflour.

palm: also called nam tan pip, jaggery, jawa or gula melaka; made from sap of sugar palm tree. Light brown to black in colour; sold in rock-hard cakes.

taco seasoning mix packaged spicy seasoning mix.

tomato

cherry: also called Tiny Tim or Tom Thumb; small and round.

egg: also called plum or roma; smallish and oval in shape.

semi-dried: partially dried tomato pieces in olive oil.

tortilla thin, round unleavened bread originating in Mexico; can be purchased frozen, fresh or vacuum-packed. Two kinds are available – one made from wheat flour, the other, corn.

turkish bread also known as pide. Comes in long (about 45cm) flat loaves as well as individual rounds; made from wheat flour.

vermicelli noodles also known as sen mee, mei fun or bee hoon; long noodle made with rice flour.

vinegar

balsamic: authentic only from Modena, Italy. Made from wine of white Trebbiano grapes specially processed then aged in antique wooden casks.

red wine: based on fermented red wine.

rice: a colourless vinegar made from fermented rice and flavoured with sugar and salt. Also known as seasoned rice vinegar.

white: made from spirit of cane sugar.

white wine: made from white wine.

water chestnuts resembles chestnut in appearance; small brown tubers with a crisp, white, nutty-tasting flesh. Available in cans from supermarkets.

yeast allow 2 teaspoons (7g) dried granulated yeast to each 15g fresh yeast.

zucchini also known as courgette.

index

facts & figures

These conversions are approximate only, but the difference between an exact and the approximate conversion of various liquid and dry measures is minimal and will not affect your cooking results.

Note: NZ, Canada, US and UK all use 15ml tablespoons. Australian tablespoons measure 20ml. All cup and spoon measurements are level.

Measuring equipment
The difference between one country's measuring cups and another's is, at most, within a 2 or 3 teaspoon variance. (For the record, 1 Australian metric measuring cup holds approximately 250ml.) The most accurate way of measuring dry ingredients is to weigh them. For liquids, use a clear glass or plastic jug having metric markings.

How to measure
When using graduated measuring cups, shake dry ingredients loosely into the appropriate cup. Do not tap the cup on a bench or tightly pack the ingredients unless directed to do so. Level the top of measuring cups and measuring spoons with a knife. When measuring liquids, place a clear glass or plastic jug having metric markings on a flat surface to check accuracy at eye level.

Dry measures

metric	imperial
15g	½oz
30g	1oz
60g	2oz
90g	3oz
125g	4oz (¼lb)
155g	5oz
185g	6oz
220g	7oz
250g	8oz (½lb)
280g	9oz
315g	10oz
345g	11oz
375g	12oz (¾lb)
410g	13oz
440g	14oz
470g	15oz
500g	16oz (1lb)
750g	24oz (1½lb)
1kg	32oz (2lb)

We use large eggs with an average weight of 60g.

Liquid measures

metric	imperial
30 ml	1 fluid oz
60 ml	2 fluid oz
100 ml	3 fluid oz
125 ml	4 fluid oz
150 ml	5 fluid oz (¼ pint/1 gill)
190 ml	6 fluid oz
250 ml (1cup)	8 fluid oz
300 ml	10 fluid oz (½ pint)
500 ml	16 fluid oz
600 ml	20 fluid oz (1 pint)
1000 ml (1litre)	1¾ pints

Helpful measures

metric	imperial
3mm	⅛in
6mm	¼in
1cm	½in
2cm	¾in
2.5cm	1in
6cm	2½in
8cm	3in
20cm	8in
23cm	9in
25cm	10in
30cm	12in (1ft)

Oven temperatures
These oven temperatures are only a guide for conventional ovens. For fan-forced ovens, check the manufacturer's manual.

	°C (Celsius)	°F (Fahrenheit)	Gas Mark
Very slow	120	250	½
Slow	150	275 – 300	1 – 2
Moderately slow	160	325	3
Moderate	180	350 – 375	4 – 5
Moderately hot	200	400	6
Hot	220	425 – 450	7 – 8
Very hot	240	475	9

ARE YOU MISSING SOME OF THE WORLD'S FAVOURITE COOKBOOKS?

The Australian Women's Weekly cookbooks are available from bookshops, cookshops, supermarkets and other stores all over the world. You can also buy direct from the publisher, using the order form below.

Mini Series £2.50 190x138mm 64 pages			
	QTY		QTY
4 Fast Ingredients		Italian	
15-minute Feasts		Jams & Jellies	
30-minute Meals		Kids' Party Food	
50 Fast Chicken Fillets		Last-minute Meals	
After-work Stir-fries		Lebanese Cooking	
Barbecue		Malaysian Favourites	
Barbecue Chicken		Microwave	
Barbecued Seafood		Mince	
Biscuits, Brownies & Biscotti		Muffins	
Bites		Noodles	
Bowl Food		Party Food	
Burgers, Rösti & Fritters		Pasta	
Café Cakes		Pickles and Chutneys	
Cafe Food		Potatoes	
Casseroles		Risotto	
Char-grills & Barbecues		Roast	
Cheesecakes, Pavlovas & Trifles		Salads	
Chocolate		Seafood	
Chocolate Cakes		Simple Slices	
Christmas Cakes & Puddings		Simply Seafood	
Cocktails		Skinny Food	
Curries		Stir-fries	
Drinks		Summer Salads	
Fast Fish		Tapas, Antipasto & Mezze	
Fast Food for Friends		Thai Cooking	
Fast Soup		Thai Favourites	
Finger Food		Vegetarian	
From the Shelf		Vegetarian Stir-fries	
Gluten-free Cooking		Vegie Main Meals	
Ice-creams & Sorbets		Wok	
Indian Cooking		**TOTAL COST**	**£**

NAME

ADDRESS

POSTCODE

DAYTIME PHONE

I ENCLOSE MY CHEQUE/MONEY ORDER FOR £

OR PLEASE CHARGE MY VISA, ACCESS OR MASTERCARD NUMBER

CARDHOLDER'S NAME

EXPIRY DATE

CARDHOLDER'S SIGNATURE

To order: Mail or fax – photocopy or complete the order form above, and send your credit card details or cheque payable to: Australian Consolidated Press (UK), Moulton Park Business Centre, Red House Road, Moulton Park, Northampton NN3 6AQ, phone (+44) (01) 604 497531, fax (+44) (01) 604 497533, e-mail books@acpuk.com. Or order online at **www.acpuk.com**
Non-UK residents: We accept the credit cards listed on the coupon, or cheques, drafts or International Money Orders payable in sterling and drawn on a UK bank. Credit card charges are at the exchange rate current at the time of payment.
Postage and packing UK: Add £1.00 per order plus 25p per book.
Postage and packing overseas: Add £2.00 per order plus 50p per book.
Offer ends 31.12.2006

Food director Pamela Clark
Food editor Louise Patniotis
Nutritional information Angela Muscat
ACP BOOKS
Editorial director Susan Tomnay
Creative director Hieu Chi Nguyen
Senior editor Julie Collard
Designer Josii Do
Sales director Brian Cearnes
Brand manager Renée Crea
Production manager Carol Currie
Chief executive officer John Alexander
Group publisher Pat Ingram
Publisher Sue Wannan
Editorial director (AWW) Deborah Thomas
Produced by ACP Books, Sydney.
Printing by Times Printers, Singapore.
Published by ACP Publishing Pty Limited,
54 Park St. Sydney;
GPO Box 4088, Sydney, NSW 2001.
Ph: (02) 9282 8618 Fax: (02) 9267 9438.
acpbooks@acp.com.au
www.acpbooks.com.au
To order books phone 136 116.
Send recipe enquiries to
Recipeenquiries@acp.com.au

Laura Bamford, Director ACP Books.
lbamford@acplon.co.uk
Ph: +44 (207) 812 6526
Australia Distributed by Network Services,
GPO Box 4088, Sydney, NSW 1028.
Ph: (02) 9282 8777 Fax: (02) 9264 3278.
United Kingdom Distributed by Australian
Consolidated Press (UK), Moulton Park Business
Centre, Red House Road, Moulton Park,
Northampton, NN3 6AQ. Ph: (01604) 497 531
Fax: (01604) 497 533 acpuktld@aol.com
Canada Distributed by Whitecap Books Ltd,
351 Lynn Ave, North Vancouver, BC, V7J 2C4
Ph: (604) 980 9852 Fax: (604) 980 8197
customerservice@whitecap.ca
www.whitecap.ca
New Zealand Distributed by Netlink Distribution
Company, ACP Media Centre, Cnr Fanshawe
and Beaumont Streets, Westhaven, Auckland.
PO Box 47906, Ponsonby, Auckland, NZ.
Ph: (9) 366 9966 ask@ndcnz.co.nz
South Africa Distributed by PSD Promotions,
30 Diesel Road, Isando, Gauteng, Johannesb
PO Box 1175, Isando, 1600, Gauteng, Johanne
Ph: (27 11) 392 6065/7 Fax: (27 11) 392 6079
orders@psdprom.co.za

Clark, Pamela.
The Australian Women's Weekly
Outdoor Eating

Includes index.
ISBN 1 86396 505 X

1. Outdoor cookery. I. Title.
II. Title: Australian Women's Weekly.

641.578

© ACP Publishing Pty Limited 2005
ABN 18 053 273 546

This publication is copyright. No part of it may
reproduced or transmitted in any form without
written permission of the publishers.

Cover Steak and aïoli open sandwiches, pa
Stylist Marie-Helene Clauzon
Photographer Brett Stevens
Back cover at left, Onion and anchovy tartle
page 14; at right, Seafood skewers with radic
and fennel salad, page 30.